PLANET EARTH

Illustrations and infographics
by Federica Fragapane

Text
by Chiara Piroddi

TABLE OF CONTENTS

HERE I AM!

Let me introduce myself: my name is **Benjamin Tard,**
but everyone calls me **Ben.**
I'm a *tardigrade*, I travel the world
and explore its secrets.

DO YOU KNOW WHAT A TARDIGRADE IS?

My name means "slow stepper",
but I'm also known as a water bear or moss piglet.

I belong to a rare species of *invertebrates*, the Tardigrada,
and **in the animal world** I'm considered a true **superhero**
because I'm able to survive in any environment, even under the most
extreme conditions!

For example, I could plunge into a pot of boiling water, hide inside the
freezer, bathe in pure alcohol, live
ten years without water, and even be launched into space:
I would still survive!
I'm not surprised that you haven't seen me before; I'm very small, let's say
more or less the size of a grain of sand, yet I'm almost invincible!

*Curiosity, perseverance and the ability to adapt
to any situation,
are the distinguishing features that make me
a perfect explorer.*

The world is a special place that has always fascinated and aroused the
curiosity of those who travel and study it,
and are driven by a thirst for
insatiable knowledge.

I intend to follow in their footsteps and set off on a journey
that will lead me to discover the **secrets of our planet**.

Are you brave enough to come along?

GOOD: 3,2,1... LET'S GO!

Minimum and maximum
temperature
in which I can survive

-460°F
(-272°C)

300°F
(150°C)

Maximum
height
0.2 in
(0.5 mm)

1150

Number
of recorded
species

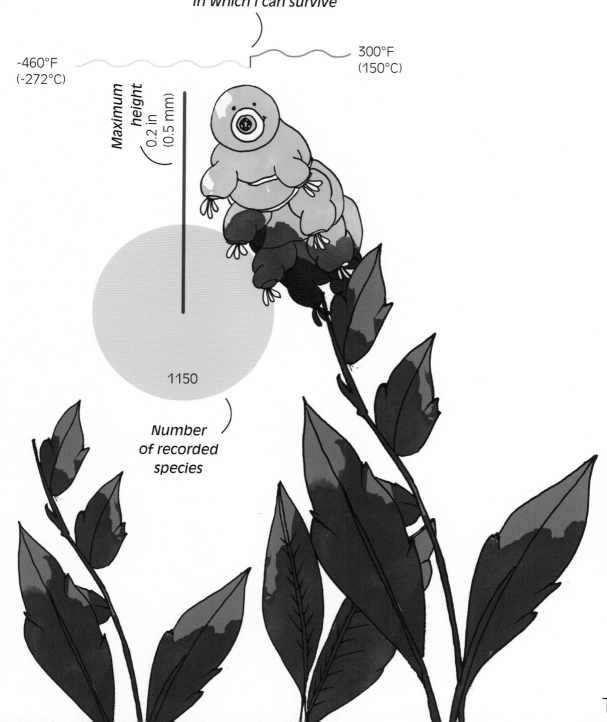

BEFORE WE BEGIN...

You should know that in this book you will find an interesting and original story about how the world is formed.

Surely at school you will would come across various descriptions of our planet. Some might have been interesting and compelling, while others might have been lengthy and filled with complex, scientific facts: pages and pages of hard-to-read text.

WHAT IF I TOLD YOU THAT IT WAS POSSIBLE TO LEARN EVEN THE MOST COMPLICATED DATA AT A GLANCE?

What if numbers were shapes, dots and lines that spread across the page, conveying details and measurements about the most complex ideas, in an intuitive way?

And what if the text was short, simple and even a bit playful, scattered with drawings?

Thanks to a special and original communication tool called infographics, discovering and exploring the world is no longer difficult or boring.

Infographics enable us to express ideas through images.

Rather than being written, the numeric data is expressed in original and easy-to-understand graphs that are enriched with colorful illustrations.
Additionally, special symbols such as geometrical shapes, rising lines or colored circles are used to visually convey the information.

In this way, to find out which one is faster between the cheetah and the peregrine falcon, all you have to do is glance at the size of the fan lines next to each animal. Or, if you want to find out whether the Arabian Desert is larger than the Kalahari, simply look at the size of the pink dot next to each.

Exploring our planet is therefore fast and intuitive, and interesting facts are easily memorized because our memory retains images more easily than words.

Chapter after chapter we'll discover how the world is made and how it's populated: its peculiarities, its strangest inhabitants, the climate of various environments, the areas in which humans have nurtured animals and those in which they have been neglected.

First we'll launch into space to discover the portion of the universe that our planet is part of: the *Solar System*.

We'll therefore view the *Earth from above*. We can then observe the distance between our planet and the Moon, as well as the size and thickness of its layers.

Returning home across the *Atmosphere* we'll consider the speed of some meteorological phenomena; for example: is hail quicker than a tornado?

After landing, we'll discover the incredible variety of animal species that inhabit the planet, besides those that are yet to be discovered!

Then we'll take a look at the unique characteristics of *the Earth's natural environments*, for example, we'll discover how the mountains were formed and what happens in the depths of the ocean.

We'll venture into the largest forests in the world, advancing among the plants and the animals that populate them. We'll also go to seemingly uninhabited regions to discover the characteristics of the unique life forms that live in the grasslands, the steppes and the largest deserts, both those which are sunburned as well as those buried in ice.

Just by glancing at the symbols, we'll learn about some of Mother Nature's great achievements: the highest peaks, the fiery giants, the longest rivers and the deepest lakes.

Finally, by comparing the abilities of some of the most talented jumpers, runners and weight lifters, I'll show you that I'm not the only *superhero in the animal world*.

This is our itinerary, which by the way, can totally be turned on its head! In fact, you can browse the book in whatever order you prefer.

THERE ARE NO RULES OTHER THAN TO FOLLOW YOUR CURIOSITY
AND LET IT BE YOUR GUIDE!

CHAPTER 1

Orbital velocity

Mass

Length
of one day

Number of moons

Median temperature (above zero)

Median temperature (below zero)

CHAPTER 2

Revolution period

Rotation period

Radius

Mass

Orbital velocity

Maximum temperature

Thickness

Percentage of each layer's volume
compared to the Earth's total volume

CHAPTER 3

Altitude

Median temperature

Median speed

Maximum size recorded

CHAPTER 4

Percentage of animal species that are
thought to be unknown

Known animal species

Maximum height or length in the category

CHAPTER 5

Height

CHAPTER 6

Volume

Depth of the layer

Pressure

Temperature

CHAPTER 7

Total volume

Continents

Percentage of fresh water on individual continents

Maximum depth

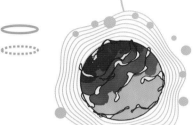

CHAPTER 8

Maximum and minimum temperature

Maximum and minimum rainfall

Median height of plants

Number of animal
species recorded

Expanse of forest

CHAPTER 9

Maximum and minimum temperature

Maximum and minimum rainfall

Median height of plants

Number of animal
species recorded

CHAPTER 10

Maximum and minimum temperature

Maximum and minimum rainfall

Median height of plants

Expanse of desert

CHAPTER 11

Maximum and minimum temperature

Maximum and minimum rainfall

Expanse

Percentage of variance
Expanse of glaciers

Depth of the ice

CHAPTER 12

Height

Length

Rate of flow

Area

Speed

Strength

Height reached

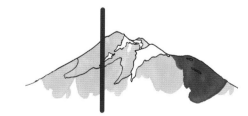

*The animals that you'll see portrayed beside the habitats in which they live,
were chosen as typical examples of those environments.*

11

Walrus

Polar
Bear

Black
Catfish

Lanternfish

**NORTH
AMERICA**

Giant
squid

*ATLANTIC
OCEAN*

Porpoise

Ara

*Amazon
River*

Toco
Toucan

*PACIFIC
OCEAN*

**SOUTH
AMERICA**

Rüppell's
Vulture

LLullaillaco

*Cerro Tipas
Ojos
del Salado*

Pelican
Eel

Emperor
Penguin

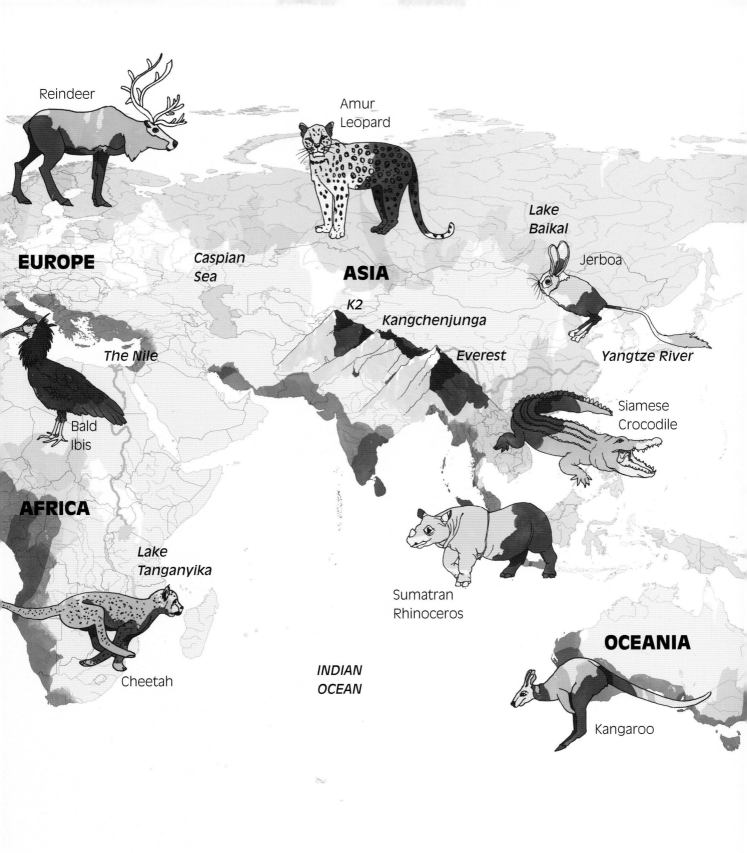

Reindeer

Amur Leopard

Lake Baikal

Jerboa

EUROPE

Caspian Sea

ASIA

K2

Kangchenjunga

Everest

Yangtze River

The Nile

Bald Ibis

Siamese Crocodile

AFRICA

Lake Tanganyika

Cheetah

Sumatran Rhinoceros

OCEANIA

INDIAN OCEAN

Kangaroo

CHAPTER I

THE PLANETS OF THE SOLAR SYSTEM

Have you ever looked up at the starry sky to admire the multitude of bright specks illuminating it, and asked yourself: *I wonder what goes on up there?*

At hundreds, thousands and millions of light years above our heads, there are stars and planets moving, flipping and tumbling through Space.
The **Sun** is one of these stars. Its gravitational force keeps several celestial objects, which are part of the **Solar System** in its orbit, including the **Earth**.

The Solar System is kind of an enormous, irregular-shaped sphere with a diameter of about 80 au, Astronomical Units, a measure that is roughly
7 thousand 450 million miles (12 thousand million kilometers)!

Beside the **planets** and their respective moons, it includes smaller bodies like **asteroids** and **comets**, and finally dust, gas and particles that comprise the **cosmic dust**.

The first time humans were able to venture into space was
on April 12, 1961 with a mission named *Vostok 1*, which was undertaken by the very brave Russian cosmonaut, *Yuri Gagarin*, whom everyone watched with bated breath.

It was he who first stated that, seen from above, the Earth was blue!

mass

orbital velocity

(speed at which
the planet orbits
around the Sun)

THE PLANETS OF THE SOLAR SYSTEM

As you know, the Earth is part of
the **Solar System.**

OUTER SOLAR SYSTEM

JUPITER   SUN

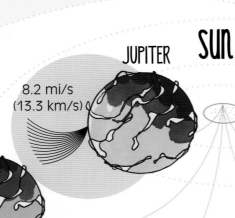

8.2 mi/s
(13.3 km/s)

SATURN

6 mi/s
(9.7 km/

4.2 mi/s
(6.8 km/s)

URANUS

NEPTUNE

3.3 mi/s
(5.4 km/s)

The Solar System comprises all *astronomical objects*,
which are made from different materials,
from the stars that revolve around the Sun.

Astronomical objects or celestial
objects are: satellites, asteroids,
comets, meteoroids and of course the
planets, which are kept in orbit by the
Sun's gravitational force.

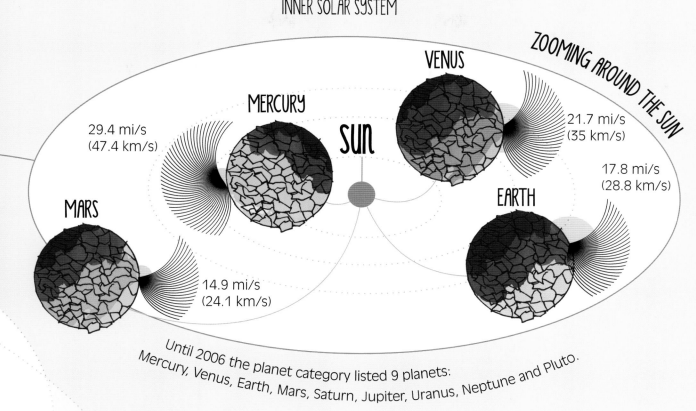

INNER SOLAR SYSTEM

ZOOMING AROUND THE SUN

VENUS

MERCURY

SUN

21.7 mi/s
(35 km/s)

17.8 mi/s
(28.8 km/s)

29.4 mi/s
(47.4 km/s)

EARTH

MARS

14.9 mi/s
(24.1 km/s)

Until 2006 the planet category listed 9 planets:
Mercury, Venus, Earth, Mars, Saturn, Jupiter, Uranus, Neptune and Pluto.

However, in 2006 the International Astronomical Union (IAU) removed **Pluto** from the planet category and listed it under the **dwarf planets**. Since then, the official number of planets is **eight!**

PLUTO

2.9 mi/s
(4.7 km/s)

(dwarf planet)

Rocky planets

Gaseous planets

The planets that are the **furthest** from the Sun are also the slowest.

Pluto, for example, is ten times slower than Mercury, which is the closest planet to the Sun.

10 hours

11 hours

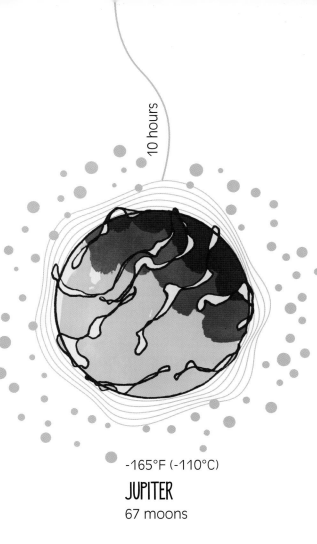

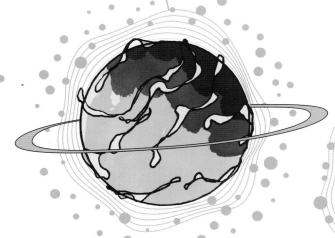

-165°F (-110°C)

JUPITER
67 moons

-220 °F (-140°C)

SATURN
62 moons

-320°F
(-195°C)

URANUS
27 moons

Mercury, Venus, Earth and Mars are **rocky planets,** because they are mainly composed of rock and metal, and they belong to the *internal solar system*.

On the other hand, the planets Jupiter, Saturn, Uranus and Neptune, are **gas giants** because they are mainly composed of gases and are part of the *outer solar system*.

**understanding
the symbols**

*duration of
one day*

number of moons

*median temperature
(above zero)*

*median temperature
(below zero)*

Venus, Mars, Jupiter and Saturn are visible to the naked eye, while Uranus, Neptune and Pluto can only be seen with a *telescope*.

17 hours

16 hours

24 hours

2802 hours

4223 hours

25 hours

153 hours

-330°F (-200°C)
NEPTUNE
14 moons

59°F (15°C)
EARTH
1 moon

-85°F (-65°C)
MARS
2 moons

The solar system
extends for over
*3.7 billion miles (6 billion
kilometers)*, which means
that to travel its entire
distance would be like
traveling by plane from
Milan to New York
**1 million
times!**

867°F
(464°C)
VENUS
0 moons

-373°F (-225°C)
PLUTO
5 moons

332°F (167°C)
MERCURY
0 moons

19

CHAPTER 2
PLANET EARTH

We have now landed on the planet that is best known to man,
and which has been studied in all its facets: **the Earth.**
Earth is the third planet in the solar system, as well as the largest
of the rocky planets and the only one that's inhabited.
It's a few years old by now: in fact, it was created roughly
4 and a half billion years ago!

Our home is an *extraordinary planet* thanks to its characteristics,
which seem to have been perfectly designed at the hand
of an accurate engineer who developed the magic combination
for the creation of the single most precious thing: **life**!

understanding the symbols

⬭ *revolution period*

 orbital velocity

⟅ *maximum temperature in each layer*

⬭ *rotation period*

⚪ *mass*

⚪ *percentage of volume of each layer based on the Earth's total volume*

▮ *thickness of the layer*

EARTH AND MOON

REVOLUTION PERIOD

For the **Moon**, it's the time taken to complete its orbit around the Earth.

For the **Earth**, it's the time taken to complete its orbit around the Sun.

365 days

24 hours

EARTH *radius* 3959 mi (6371 km)

27.3 days

27.3 days

ROTATION PERIOD

It takes the **Earth** 24 hours to rotate on its axis, its *rotation period* is therefore 24 hours.

On the other hand, it takes the **Moon** 27.3 days to rotate on its axis.

MOON *radius* 1079 mi (1737 km)

distance
238,600 mi
(384,000 km)

1.6 x 10²³ lb
(0.07x10²⁴ kg)

1.3 x 10²⁵ lb
(5.9x10²⁴ kg)

635,04 mi/s (1022 km/s)

18.5 mi/s (29.8 km/s)

The **Moon** is the heavenly body most easily visible to the naked eye! It's peculiarity is that it faces the Earth by always showing the **same side**.

This happens because the Moon takes 27.3 days to both rotate on its axis and orbit around the Earth.

The side of the **Earth** that faces the **Sun** is *day*, while the opposite side is *night*.

This is why when it's daytime in Europe, it's nighttime in Oceania and vice versa.

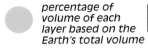

Let's try to imagine the Earth as a giant peach: the "peel" covering it is the **crust**.

Planet **Earth** is not limited to the surface supporting our feet, but *contains several inner layers.*

The *"pulp"* that immediately follows, is the **mantle** (which is divided into the upper and the lower mantle).

The *"stone"* is the Earth's **core**, which is divided into the outer core and the inner core.

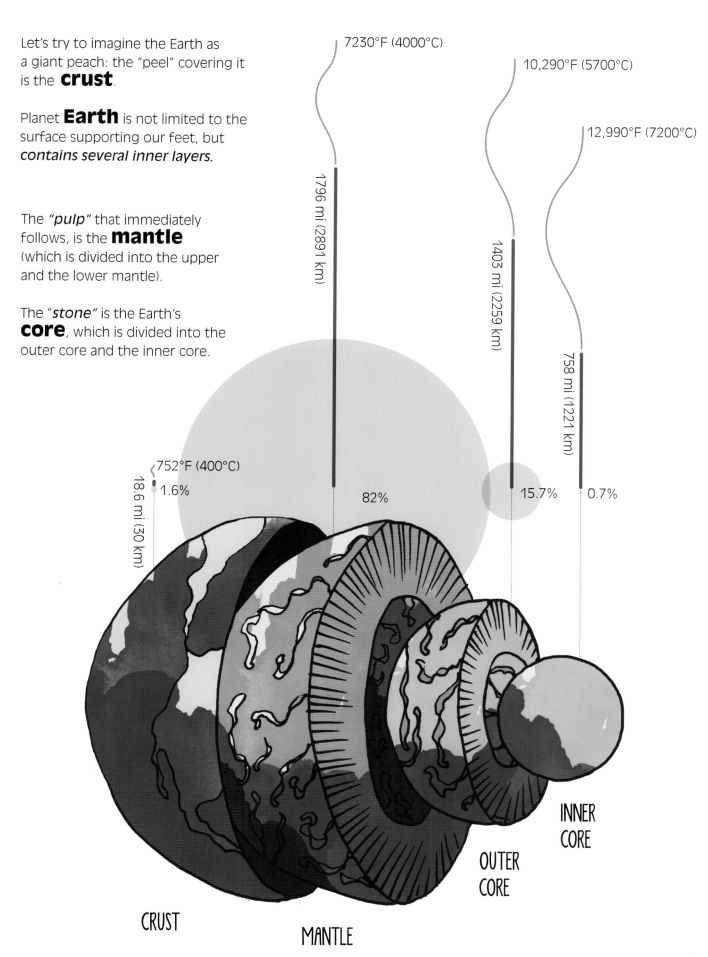

7230°F (4000°C)

10,290°F (5700°C)

12,990°F (7200°C)

1796 mi (2891 km)

1403 mi (2259 km)

758 mi (1221 km)

752°F (400°C)

18.6 mi (30 km)

1.6%

82%

15.7%

0.7%

CRUST

MANTLE

OUTER CORE

INNER CORE

CHAPTER 3

THE ATMOSPHERE

The existence of life on **Earth** is not coincidental.
In fact, a very specific set of circumstances had
to take place on our planet, to enable
the development of all living things:
the most important one
is the **atmosphere.**

This thin layer is a mixture of gases (*vapor, oxygen,
carbon dioxide*) that extend from the ground
up to about 620 mi (1000 km) in altitude. The
atmosphere's structure is complex and is divided
into layers called **"spheres"**.

The atmosphere's lowest layer is
the most dense and is about 7.4 mi (12 km) high;
this is the layer in which we find the **weather**
and the air we breathe.

The atmosphere plays a very important role:
it acts as a **shield** that filters the Sun's radiation,
and enables the metabolic processes
of many species.
*This is the reason why humans should be
taking greater care of it!*

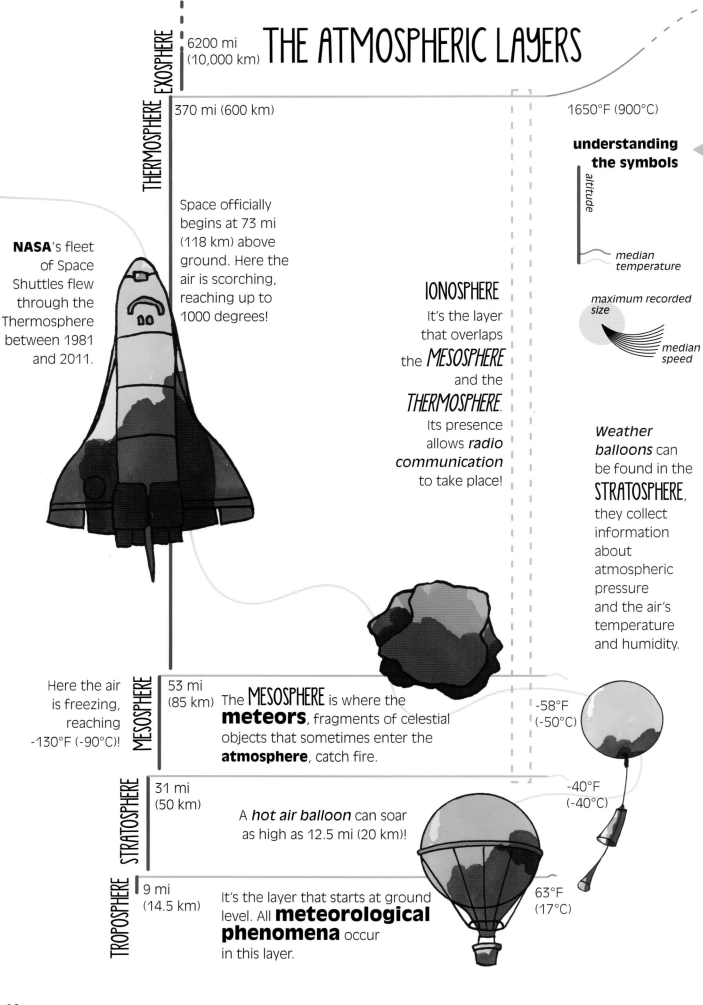

THE ATMOSPHERIC LAYERS

EXOSPHERE 6200 mi (10,000 km)

THERMOSPHERE 370 mi (600 km) — 1650°F (900°C)

understanding the symbols

altitude

median temperature

maximum recorded size

median speed

NASA's fleet of Space Shuttles flew through the Thermosphere between 1981 and 2011.

Space officially begins at 73 mi (118 km) above ground. Here the air is scorching, reaching up to 1000 degrees!

IONOSPHERE
It's the layer that overlaps the *MESOSPHERE* and the *THERMOSPHERE*. Its presence allows *radio communication* to take place!

Weather balloons can be found in the STRATOSPHERE, they collect information about atmospheric pressure and the air's temperature and humidity.

MESOSPHERE 53 mi (85 km)

Here the air is freezing, reaching -130°F (-90°C)!

The MESOSPHERE is where the **meteors**, fragments of celestial objects that sometimes enter the **atmosphere**, catch fire.

-58°F (-50°C)

STRATOSPHERE 31 mi (50 km) — -40°F (-40°C)

A *hot air balloon* can soar as high as 12.5 mi (20 km)!

TROPOSPHERE 9 mi (14.5 km)

It's the layer that starts at ground level. All **meteorological phenomena** occur in this layer.

63°F (17°C)

26

METEOROLOGICAL PHENOMENA

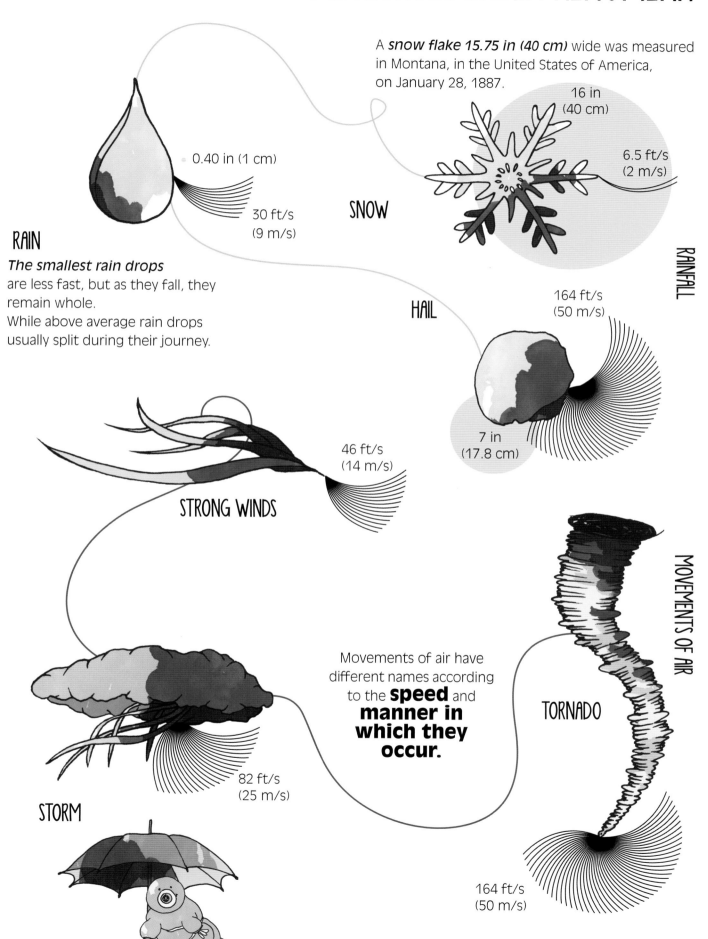

A **_snow flake 15.75 in (40 cm)_** wide was measured in Montana, in the United States of America, on January 28, 1887.

16 in (40 cm)

6.5 ft/s (2 m/s)

SNOW

0.40 in (1 cm)

30 ft/s (9 m/s)

RAINFALL

RAIN

The smallest rain drops are less fast, but as they fall, they remain whole.
While above average rain drops usually split during their journey.

HAIL

164 ft/s (50 m/s)

7 in (17.8 cm)

46 ft/s (14 m/s)

STRONG WINDS

Movements of air have different names according to the **speed** and **manner in which they occur.**

MOVEMENTS OF AIR

TORNADO

82 ft/s (25 m/s)

STORM

164 ft/s (50 m/s)

CHAPTER 4

THE ANIMAL KINGDOM

On **Earth** there is a realm that includes living beings that are *extremely diverse in shape, size and ability.*

They can be as small as a few millimeters,
or as big as a car or a building.
They are covered by thick fur, multicolored feathers or scales.
They can compete with the speed of a train, sink to incredible depths
in the ocean or rise in flight and disappear into the clouds.
Some are examples of elegance, others are creepy!
They live in the most remote places, but also in those most familiar to us,
such as our own homes.
They often live in herds, though there's no shortage of grumpy loners.
They have very specific **habits** and **behaviors** that arouse the admiration
of humans.

It's not easy to live according to the laws of this kingdom.
Its inhabitants must always be on guard to stay safe
from predators in an ongoing battle for **survival.**
Some live just a few days, others for centuries, some even seem to be
immortal.

*The animal kingdom is the most fascinating, diverse and intriguing
realm that is left to explore.*

ANIMAL SPECIES

Animals form a vast kingdom that comprises many **species**, each with its unique **characteristics.**

Maximum height or length in the category

Number of animal species that are still unknown!

Known animal species

Length of a blue whale

108 ft (33 m)

Length of a whale shark

59 ft (18 m)

MAMMALS

FISH

45,000

32,400

5613

5501

REPTILES

BIRDS

Length of a reticulated python

28.5 ft (8.7 m)

Length of an ostrich

9 ft (2.7 m)

10,483

10,064

11,933

9547

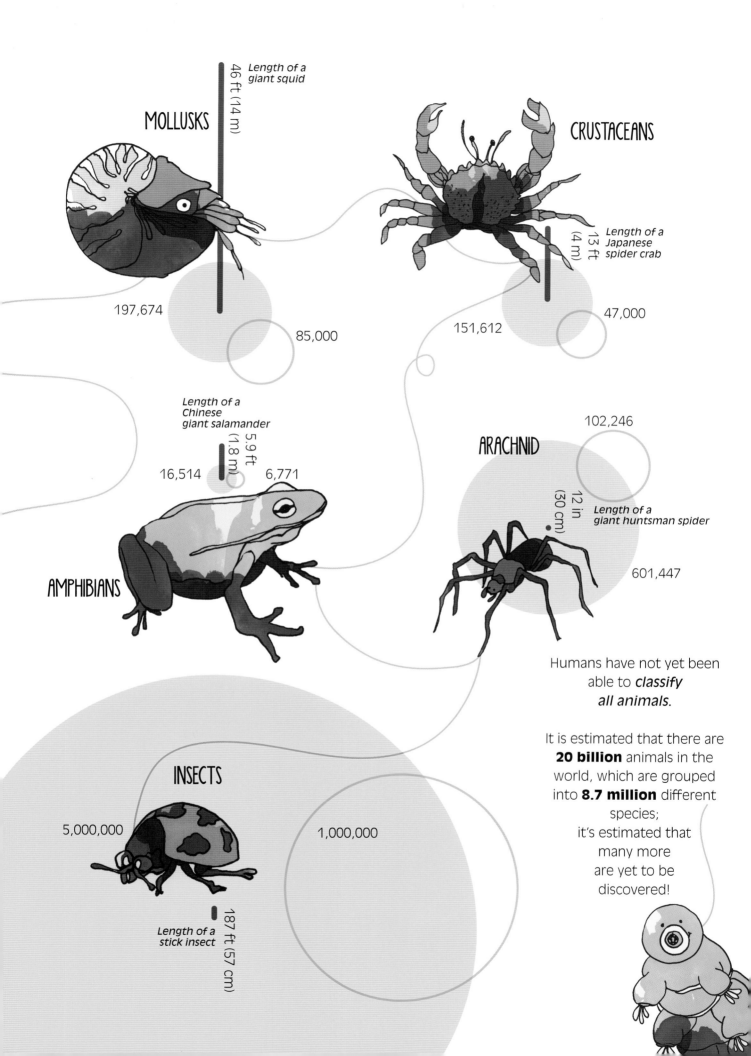

MOLLUSKS

Length of a
giant squid

46 ft (14 m)

197,674

85,000

CRUSTACEANS

Length of a
Japanese
spider crab

13 ft
(4 m)

151,612

47,000

Length of a
Chinese
giant salamander

5.9 ft
(1.8 m)

16,514

6,771

AMPHIBIANS

ARACHNID

102,246

12 in
(30 cm)

Length of a
giant huntsman spider

601,447

Humans have not yet been
able to *classify
all animals.*

It is estimated that there are
20 billion animals in the
world, which are grouped
into **8.7 million** different
species;
it's estimated that
many more
are yet to be
discovered!

INSECTS

5,000,000

1,000,000

Length of a
stick insect

187 ft (57 cm)

CHAPTER 5

MOUNTAINS

Mountains represent the memory of the **Earth**.

They are like a *thousand-year old archive*, in which the enduring history of the movements of the **Earth's crust**, the collisions between the tectonic plates, and the repeated volcanic eruptions is preserved forever, along with the action of the *wind and other weather events*, all of which have molded these **majestic giants** like dedicated craftsmen.

Mountains are a conglomerate of *earth and rock that is at least 980 ft (300 m) high*. They have always played a key role in the life of our planet. Besides being home to numerous **animal and plant species,** they have for instance, outlined the *natural boundaries* of many countries, *protecting* them from enemy invasion.

Due to their height, they are able to influence a region's **weather** pattern: blocking a storm or even causing rain.

The population in the mountains varies.
Animals have learned to cope with the low temperatures and to adapt to the hostile environment. For example **reptiles** such as vipers, which like rocks and scrub, live there. Meanwhile, the queen of the mountains, *the golden eagle*, nests on the mountain peaks together with the *white-winged snowfinch* that lives on the edge of the glaciers, and the *rock ptarmigan*, whose plumage changes with the seasons: white as snow in winter and gray-brown like the rocks in summer.

Mammals that have adapted to the high altitude also live here, such as *the Alpine marmot, the mountain hare, the short-tailed weasel* as well as *the Alpine ibex, the chamois*, and the shaggy *Tibetan yak*. Due to their hoofs, the latter are known as *ungulates*, and have come to symbolize the mountains!

TECTONIC PLATES MOVEMENTS

The **lithosphere**, that is, the layer of the Earth that consists of the crust and the upper *mantle* (these terms are explained in chapter 2), includes a number of sections called **tectonic plates,** which are in constant motion, shifting about **0.8 in (2 cm) a year.**

As they move, the *boundaries* of the plates, that is their outer edges, may *move into one another, move sideways* to one another, *or move apart*.

Major geological phenomena such as **the formation of the continents and mountains** result from the movement of the tectonic plates.

TRANSFORM PLATE BOUNDARIES

The *crust* is never created nor destroyed and the plates slide sideways in relation to each other.

TYPES OF ELEVATION

VOLCANIC MOUNTAINS

They form when molten rock *(magma)* from the depths of the **Earth** erupts through the **crust** and piles up.

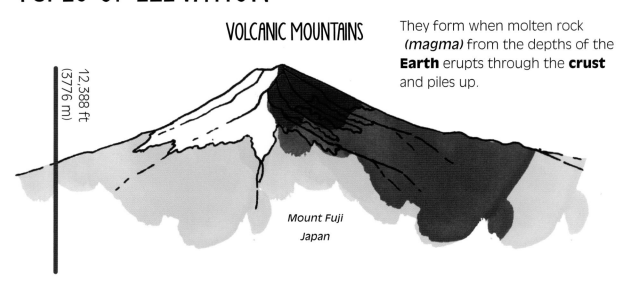

12,388 ft (3776 m)

Mount Fuji
Japan

PLATEAUS

They form when **the tectonic plates** collide and cause the ground to rise without bending or cracking, and are subsequently exposed to the *weather and erosion*.

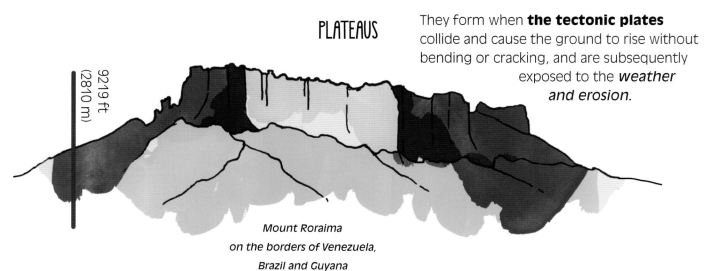

9219 ft (2810 m)

Mount Roraima
on the borders of Venezuela,
Brazil and Guyana

DIVERGENT PLATE BOUNDARIES

The plates move away from one another and the space created between them is filled by *new oceanic lithosphere.*

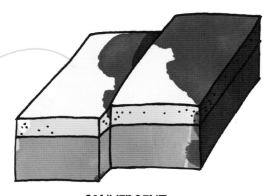

CONVERGENT PLATE BOUNDARIES

The plates move toward one another.

DOMED MOUNTAINS

When the *magma* lifts the crust, but hardens before erupting on the surface, it forms like a bubble - known as the **dome** - inside the Earth's crust.

5344 ft (1629 m)

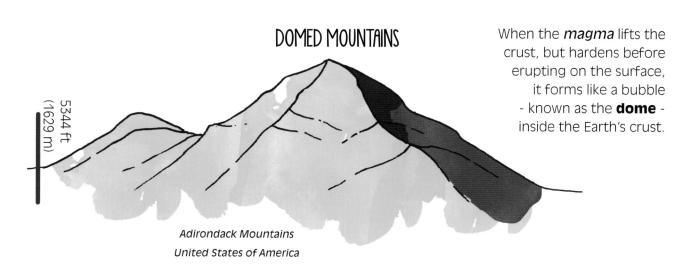

Adirondack Mountains
United States of America

14,504 ft (4421 m)

MOUNTAIN BLOCKS

They are formed when the tension within and between the **tectonic plates** causes *fractures* in the Earth's surface, pushing blocks of rock up and down (also known as *fault lines*).

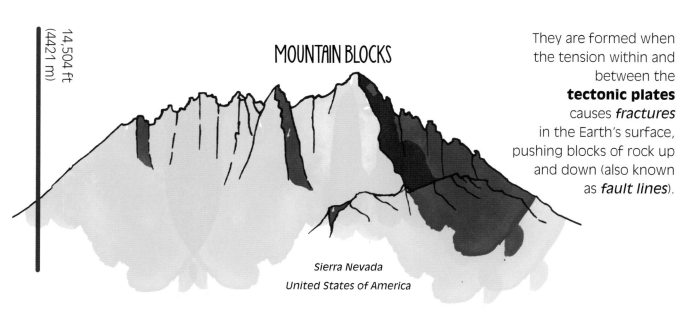

Sierra Nevada
United States of America

CHAPTER 6

OCEANS

The first time the astronauts went *into space*,
they noticed that the **Earth**, as seen from above, looked like a giant
blue sphere; that is why they called it the **Blue Planet**.

This color is due to the fact that **70% of the Earth's surface** is
covered by **oceans**: vast, fascinating and powerful giants that contain
97% of all the water on Earth.

Even our planet's **climate** is influenced by the *motion
and temperature* of the oceans, which are essential links
in **the cycle of life.**

Their dimension are: *a minimum of 930 mi (1500 km) in with for
the Atlantic, 8080 mi (13,000 km) for the Pacific, while the median
depth is about 2.5 mi (4 km).*

OCEAN STRATIFICATION

understanding the symbols

temperature minimum and maximum

pressure

(every 33 ft/10 meters of depth, there is an increase of 1 atmosphere, which is about 14.6 lb per in² /1 Kg per cm²)

68°F (20°C)

EPIPELAGIC ZONE
up to 660 ft (200 m)

This is the upper layer that is heated by the **Sun's** rays.

MESOPELAGIC ZONE
up to 3300 ft (1000 m)

39°F (4°C)   from 100 to 150 ATM

The temperature here varies greatly and *light is scarce*. The **fish** have protruding eyes, which make it easier to spot prey and predators!

355 ATM

BATHYPELAGIC ZONE
up to 13,200 ft (4000 m)

39°F (4°C)

There is no more *light* and the median *temperature* is around 39°F (4°C).

Humpback anglerfish

500 ATM

Giant squid

ABYSSAL ZONE
up to 6000 m

35F° (2°C)

HADAL ZONE
from 19,800 ft to 35,797,244 ft
(from 6000 m to 10,911 m)

This is the **deepest** zone at the bottom of the ocean.

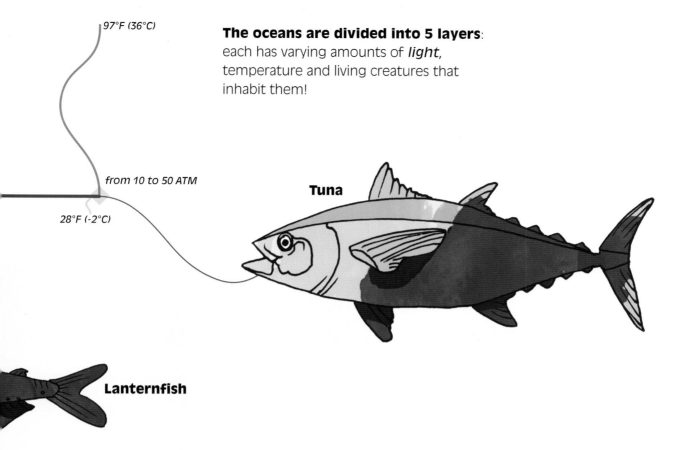

97°F (36°C)

The oceans are divided into 5 layers:
each has varying amounts of *light*,
temperature and living creatures that
inhabit them!

from 10 to 50 ATM

Tuna

28°F (-2°C)

Lanternfish

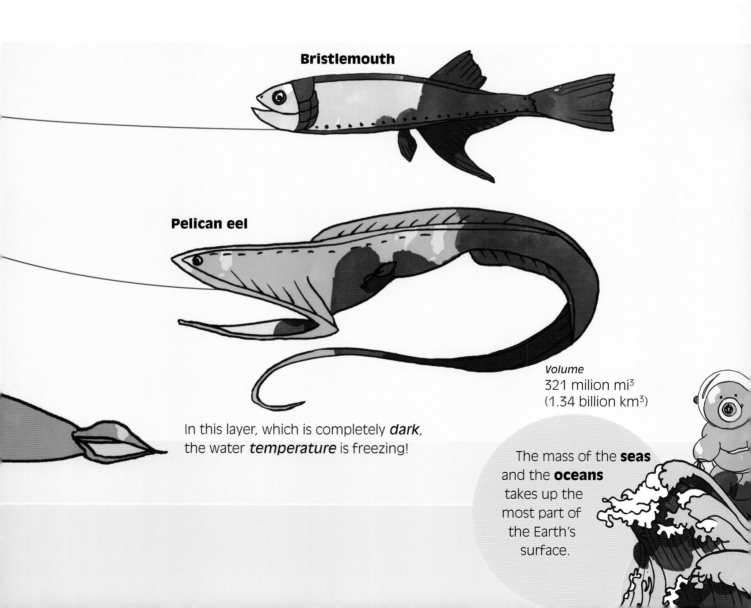

Bristlemouth

Pelican eel

Volume
321 milion mi³
(1.34 billion km³)

In this layer, which is completely *dark*,
the water *temperature* is freezing!

The mass of the **seas**
and the **oceans**
takes up the
most part of
the Earth's
surface.

CHAPTER 7

RIVERS AND LAKES

A **river** is a constant flow of water that never *runs dry*, because it is constantly being replenished by *rainfall*, the melting of *snow or glaciers* of by *groundwater*.
We are used to see it flow *on the Earth's surface*, but there are also very long underground rivers.

Lakes are depressions or basins that are filled by continental waters, that is, fresh water that flows on the *Earth's surface* and *does not originate from the sea*.
Usually, a lake has one or more **tributary rivers**, that feed the lake, and one or more **outflowing rivers** that are fed by the lake's waters.

Most of the *fresh water* on the planet; however, is not found in lakes or rivers, but is trapped inside **polar ice** and **glaciers**.
Following, in order of volume, are *groundwater*, *fresh water lakes* and finally, *rivers* (300 mi³ / 1250 km³).

FRESH WATER

Fresh water gets its name from its low salt content. Rivers, streams, lakes and underground aquifers, make up *just 3% of the Earth's water.*

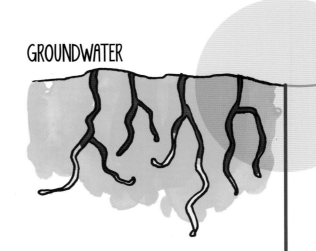

GROUNDWATER

2,028,000 mi³
(8,454,000 km³)

understanding the symbols

| maximum depth

○ total volume fresh water

○ continents

● percentage of fresh water on individual continents

SIBERIAN STURGEON

TWAIT SHAD

45%
America

TIGERFISH

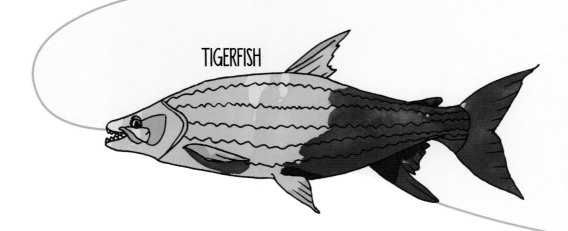

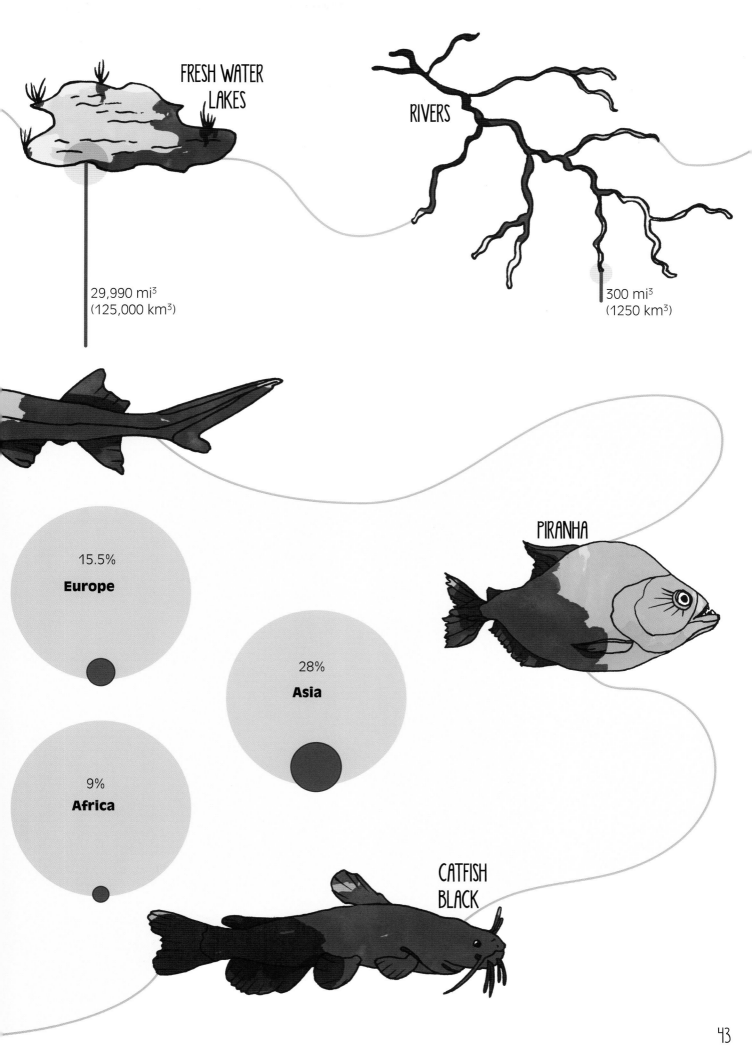

FRESH WATER
LAKES

RIVERS

29,990 mi³
(125,000 km³)

300 mi³
(1250 km³)

15.5%
Europe

28%
Asia

9%
Africa

PIRANHA

CATFISH
BLACK

CHAPTER 8

FORESTS

To go into a forest is an experience for *true explorers:*
mighty trees with soaring trunks, **multicolor animals**, **mysterious insects**,
spices and tasty **fruits**, comprise the scenery of this fantastical world.

22% of all land is covered by **forests**, among which, are the so-called **coniferous forests**
(comprised of *pine, Douglas fir, larch, citron, monkey puzzle, tsuga, cypress, sequoia etc.*),
that add up to over 35%; the **temperate broadleaf** (*oak, beech, maple,
poplar, birch, alder, chestnut, willow, olive tree etc.*) make up 15%
while the **tropical broadleaf** forests are about 50%.

The forests are an essential asset for the **Earth** and fulfill tasks of *primary
importance* for all living creatures: for example, they support the *creation of soil*
and protect it from erosion, they play a role in regulating the **rainfall**,
balance the patterns of the **wind**, and they produce **oxygen**
through the process of *photosynthesis*.
Thanks to photosynthesis, the totality of forests absorb the atmosphere's carbon dioxide,
thereby regulating the greenhouse gases and mitigating the climate.

To care for and protect this valuable resource is fundamental for the survival of the planet!

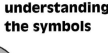

THE FORESTS AND THEIR INHABITANTS

understanding the symbols

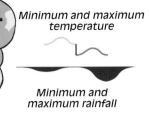

Minimum and maximum temperature

Minimum and maximum rainfall

Median height of plants

Number of registered animal species

Forest extension

Forests can be categorized according to the *species of plant that is most prevale*

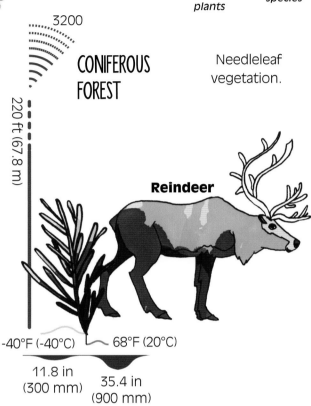

3200

CONIFEROUS FOREST

Needleleaf vegetation.

220 ft (67.8 m)

Reindeer

-40°F (-40°C)   68°F (20°C)

11.8 in (300 mm)   35.4 in (900 mm)

FORESTS WITH DECIDUOUS PLANTS

So called because they shed their leaves in the fall.

4400

79 ft (24 m)

Bald eagle

-22°F (-30°C)   86°F (30°C)

29.5 in (750 mm)   59 in (1500 mm)

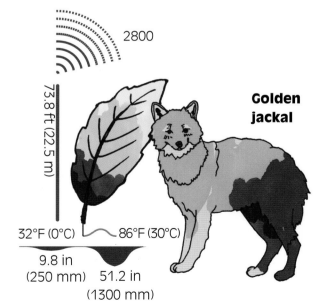

2800

73.8 ft (22.5 m)

Golden jackal

32°F (0°C)   86°F (30°C)

9.8 in (250 mm)   51.2 in (1300 mm)

SCLEROPHYLL FORESTS

With short trees and shrubs with *thick and hard leaves.*

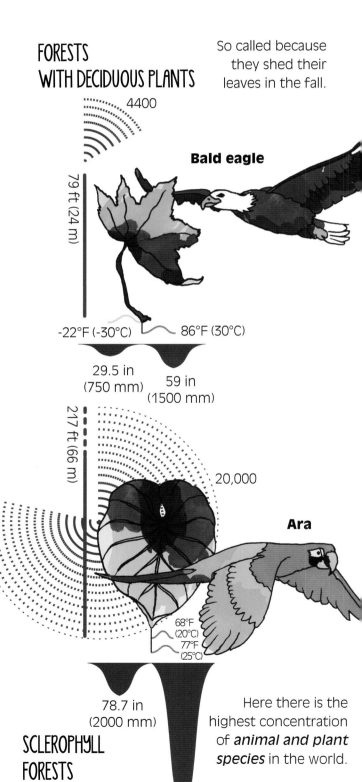

217 ft (66 m)

20,000

Ara

68°F (20°C)
77°F (25°C)

SCLEROPHYLL FORESTS

78.7 in (2000 mm)

Here there is the highest concentration of *animal and plant species* in the world.

394 in (10,000 mm)

THE 5 LARGEST FORESTS ON EARTH

1 BOREAL FOREST OR TAIGA
Canada, Europe, Northern Asia

up to 130 ft (40 m)

4,630,000 mi² (12,000,000 km²)

Siberian Tiger

Scots pine

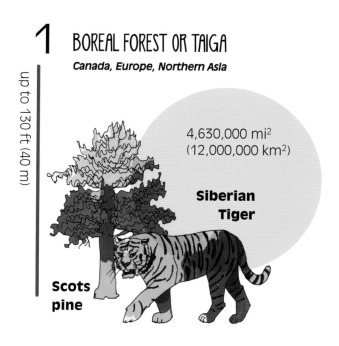

2 AMAZON FOREST
Amazon River basin in South America

98 ft (30 m)

2,700,000 mi² (7,000,000 km²)

Toco toucan

Rubber tree

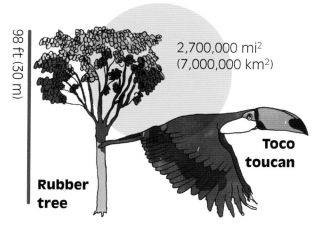

3 THICKET
The Congo

781,249 mi² (2,023,428 km²)

39 ft (12 m)

Cola acuminata

Western gorilla

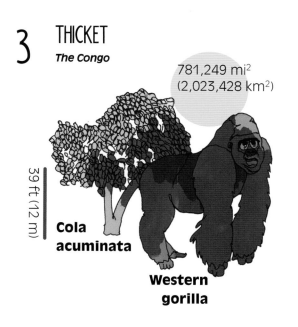

4 VALDIVIAN RAIN FOREST
Chile

115 ft (35 m)

95,790 mi² (248,100 km²)

Juan Fernandez Firecrown

Monkey puzzle tree

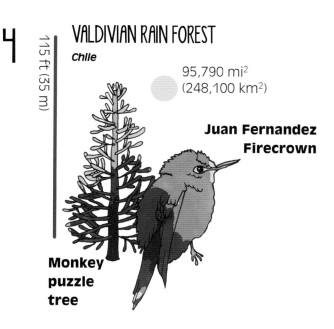

5 TONGASS NATIONAL FOREST
Alaska

115 ft (35 m)

American black bear

26,640 mi² (69,000 km²)

Western red-cedar

CHAPTER 9

SAVANNA, TEMPERATE GRASSLANDS, STEPPES

Grasslands are vast *expanses of grass*, and are populated
by various species of mammals, from **large predators** to docile **ungulates**,
as well as the most fearsome **reptiles**, all perfectly *camouflaged*
in the environment.

The majority of plants here are herbaceous and without a trunk, reaching heights
between *7.9 in (20 cm)* and *6.5 ft (2 m)*, with deep roots up to *5.9 ft (1.8 m)* long.
The **graminaceous plants**, which have a very deep root system that enables
them to survive for long periods of time *without water*,
are by far the most widespread plants in the grasslands.
A distinguishing feature of the **savannas**, on the other hand, are the **Acacias**,
in the shade of which, it is not unusual
to find a **leopard** or a pride of **lions**.

Grasslands are present across vast areas on all continents,
with the exception of Antarctica.

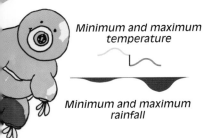

Median height of plants

Number of animal species recorded

GRASSLANDS AND THEIR INHABITANTS

There are several kinds of **grasslands** in the world that differ according to the *climate*, which also brings about *considerable differences in the vegetation*.

SAVANNA

The **savanna** is comprised of *expanses of grass* and occasional, *individual trees*.

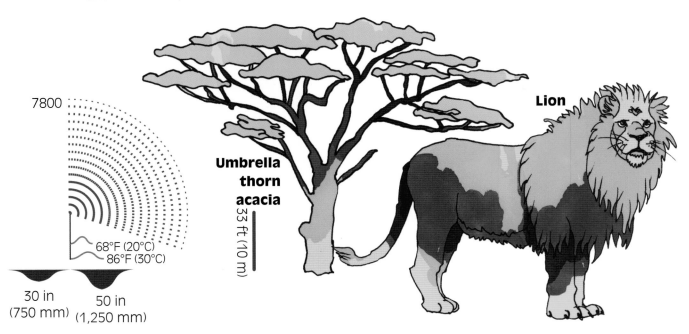

7800

68°F (20°C)
86°F (30°C)

30 in (750 mm)   50 in (1,250 mm)

Umbrella thorn acacia
33 ft (10 m)

Lion

STEPPE

Steppes for the most part are comprised by *grasses and shrubs!*

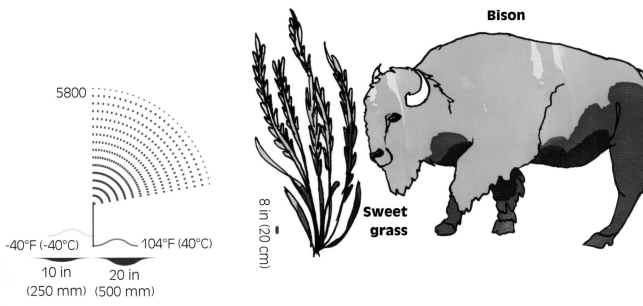

5800

-40°F (-40°C)   104°F (40°C)

10 in (250 mm)   20 in (500 mm)

8 in (20 cm)

Sweet grass

Bison

TEMPERATE GRASSLANDS

Temperate grasslands are characterized by *expanses of grass* that constitute the most prevalent vegetation!
They are categorized into the North American plains, the Australian outback, the African veld, and the South American pampas.

3300

-40°F (-40°C)   100°F (38°C)

20 in
(500 mm)

35 in
(900 mm)

NORTH AMERICAN PLAINS

Bouteloua gracilis

Red fox

8 in (20 cm)

AUSTRALIAN OUTBACK

165 ft (50 m)

Eucalyptus   **Kangaroo**

Baobab

AFRICAN VELD

50 ft (15 m)

Cheetah

SOUTH AMERICAN PAMPAS

50 ft (15 m)

Cactus   **Guanaco**

51

CHAPTER 10

SAND AND ROCK DESERTS

Deserts are real *testing grounds* for all living creatures:
the *dry climate, limited rainfall and the high salinity of the soil*
are hard challenges to overcome!

A desert is a place that has a *rainfall that is
less than 10 in (250 mm) a year*,
a number that is less than half of half the rainfall in our cities!
According to this definition, deserts aren't just those blazing expanses
of sand and rock that we usually think about, but also freezing polar lands
buried beneath permanent ice.

In both these uninhabitable environments, the vegetation struggles
to grow. Nevertheless, nature has come up with some *amazing strategies* to
enable animals and plants to *adapt* to life in such extreme conditions!

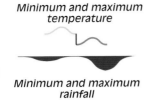

**understanding
the symbols**

Minimum and maximum
temperature

Minimum and maximum
rainfall

Median height
of plants

Expanse
of the desert

THE 5 LARGEST DESERTS IN THE WORLD

1 SAHARA

3,320,000 mi²
(8,600,000 km²)

**Date
palm**

68°F (20°C)
104°F (40°C)

4 in
(100 mm)

10 in
(250 mm)

This is the **largest** hot
desert **in the world**.
Its *dunes* can reach
heights of 590 ft (180 m)!

65 ft (20 m)

Camel

2 ARABIAN DESERT

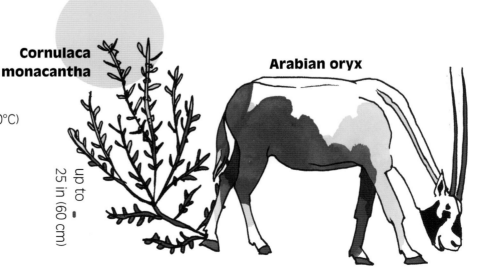

502,000 mi²
(1,300,000 km²)

**Cornulaca
monacantha**

Arabian oryx

60°F (15°C)
120°F (50°C)

1.5 in
(35 mm)

4 in
(100 mm)

It's distinguished by a vast
expanse of sand that is
mostly unexplored, and
which is called *Rub' al
Khali*.

up to
25 in (60 cm)

54

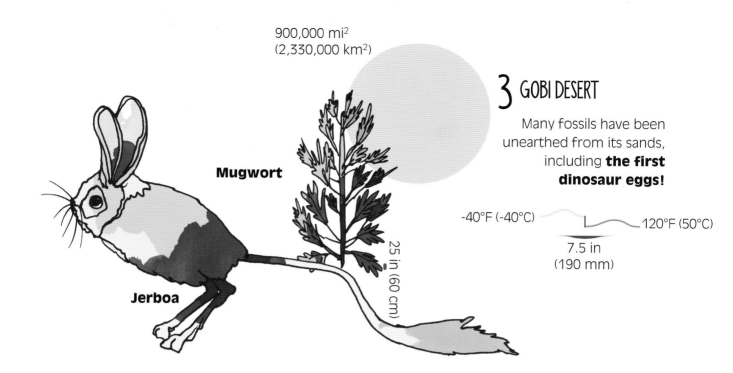

900,000 mi² (2,330,000 km²)

Mugwort

Jerboa

25 in (60 cm)

3 GOBI DESERT

Many fossils have been unearthed from its sands, including **the first dinosaur eggs!**

-40°F (-40°C) ___ 120°F (50°C)

7.5 in (190 mm)

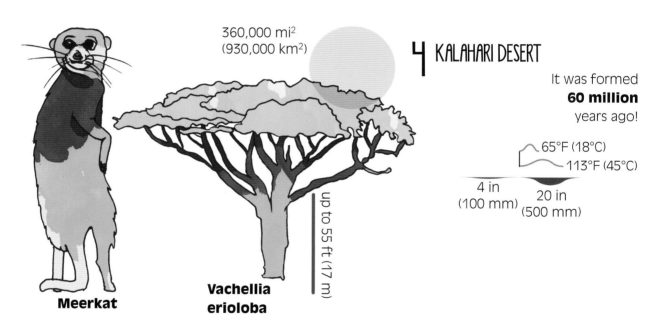

360,000 mi² (930,000 km²)

Meerkat

Vachellia erioloba

up to 55 ft (17 m)

4 KALAHARI DESERT

It was formed **60 million** years ago!

65°F (18°C)
113°F (45°C)

4 in (100 mm)   20 in (500 mm)

5 PATAGONIAN DESERT

It's the largest desert in the entire *American continent*.

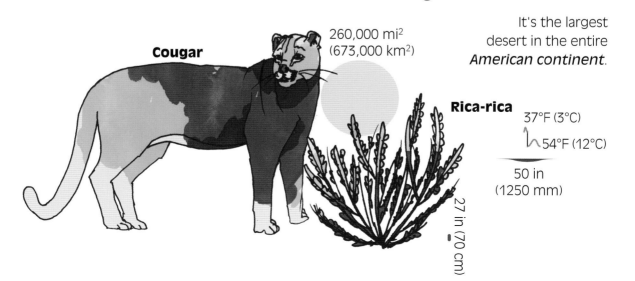

Cougar

260,000 mi² (673,000 km²)

Rica-rica

37°F (3°C)
54°F (12°C)

50 in (1250 mm)

27 in (70 cm)

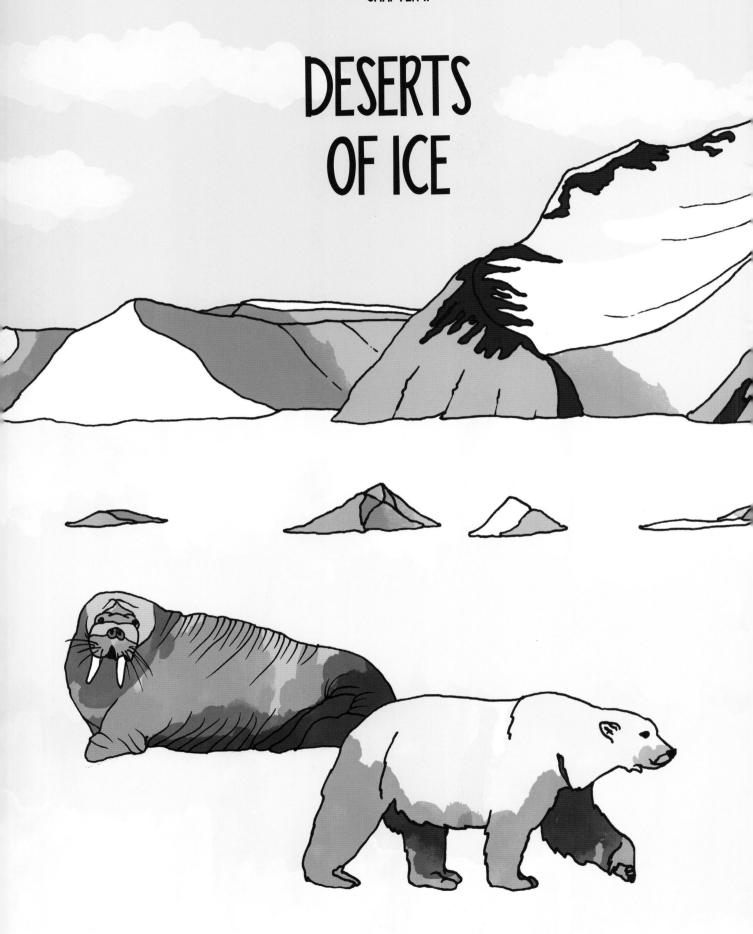

CHAPTER II

DESERTS OF ICE

The two most remote points of the Earth, the **North Pole** and the **South Pole**, are surrounded by *two large polar deserts*: the **Arctic** and the **Antarctic**.

In these icy landscapes, which are permanently covered in snow and *ice*, the *scarce rainfall* (less than 2 in -50 mm- a year), the strong *winds* and the *freezing temperatures*, mean that every living creatures' survival is tested on a daily basis. In fact, the **plant life** is limited to *lichens, mosses and algae*, while seals, penguins, polar bears, and **various species** of fish and birds, are the only animals able to withstand such harsh weather conditions.

The **Arctic** is comprised of various regions belonging to other continents (*Europe, Asia, America*) as well as a section of the *Arctic Ocean*.

Antarctica, on the other hand, is considered a continent in its own right, it is *the coldest and the most inhospitable on the planet*. The lowest temperature ever recorded on Earth is **-192°F (-89°C)** and it was measured right here on July 21, 1983!

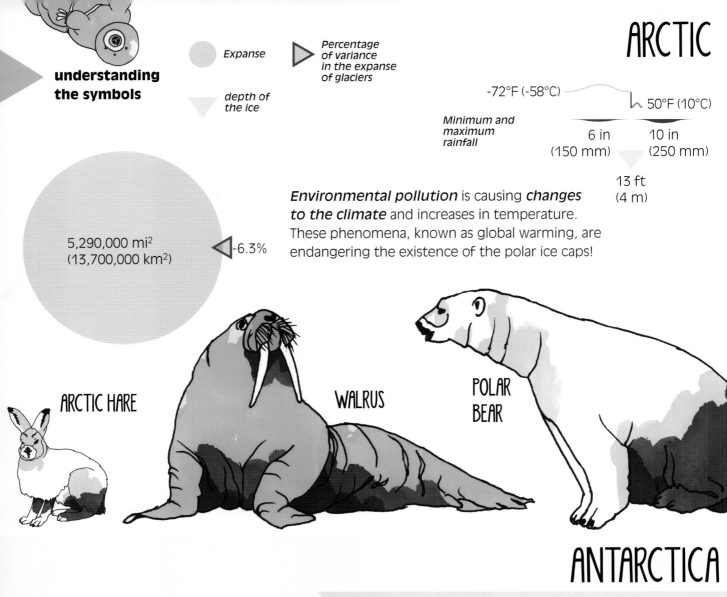

ARCTIC

understanding the symbols

Expanse

Percentage of variance in the expanse of glaciers

depth of the ice

-72°F (-58°C)   50°F (10°C)

Minimum and maximum rainfall

6 in (150 mm)   10 in (250 mm)

13 ft (4 m)

5,290,000 mi² (13,700,000 km²)   -6.3%

Environmental pollution is causing **changes to the climate** and increases in temperature. These phenomena, known as global warming, are endangering the existence of the polar ice caps!

ARCTIC HARE

WALRUS

POLAR BEAR

ANTARCTICA

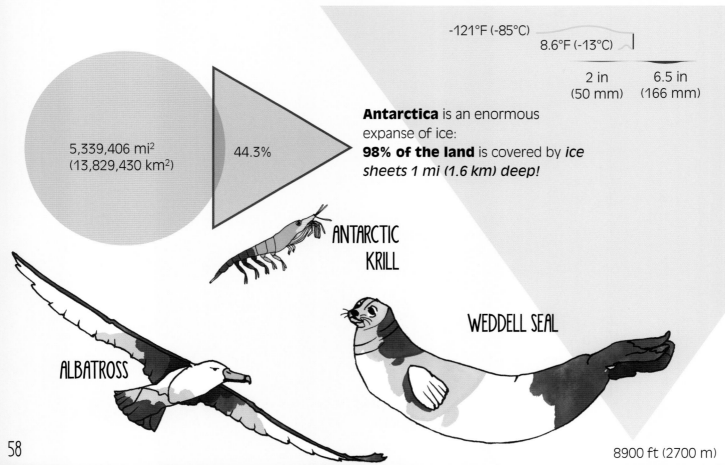

-121°F (-85°C)

8.6°F (-13°C)

2 in (50 mm)   6.5 in (166 mm)

5,339,406 mi² (13,829,430 km²)   44.3%

Antarctica is an enormous expanse of ice: **98% of the land** is covered by *ice sheets 1 mi (1.6 km) deep!*

ANTARCTIC KRILL

WEDDELL SEAL

ALBATROSS

8900 ft (2700 m)

It is thought that at this rate *the Arctic ice sheets could disappear* by 2050!

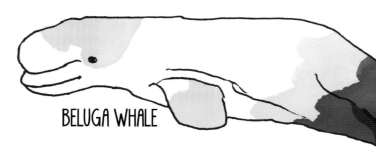

BELUGA WHALE

MUSKOX

As you can see, the two poles are very different.

Of the two, the Arctic is the more fragile, due to the warmer temperatures and the thinner ice, which is more prone to melt as a result of global warming.

To date, the Antarctic is a small island that has been spared the effects of global warming; however, if the Earth's temperatures continue to rise, over the next centuries the cold Antarctic winds and currents may no longer be able to protect our southern pole.

Unlike the Arctic, the Antarctic, *is surrounded by the Antarctic Circumpolar Current*, a cold ocean current that acts as a barrier from the other, warmer currents. This way, *the seas' temperatures are able to remain very cold*, and continue forming ice.

EMPEROR PENGUIN

ANTARCTIC MINKE WHALE

CHAPTER 12

RECORDS OF NATURE

The magnificence of **Nature**
and its inhabitants is boundless.
There are plants with *bizarre* characteristics, animals with
skills short of heroic, mountains that pierce the clouds
and rivers that flow endlessly.

Let's go on a discovery tour of some of Mother Nature's
most impressive records,
beginning with the highest peaks in the world,
then reaching the deepest abyss!

Finally, we'll witness a very exciting competition: the
animal Olympics, are about to begin!

THE HIGHEST MOUNTAINS

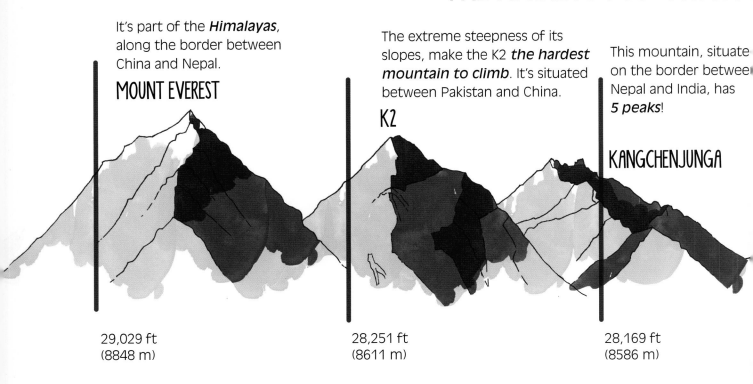

It's part of the **Himalayas**, along the border between China and Nepal.

MOUNT EVEREST

The extreme steepness of its slopes, make the K2 **the hardest mountain to climb**. It's situated between Pakistan and China.

K2

This mountain, situated on the border between Nepal and India, has **5 peaks**!

KANGCHENJUNGA

29,029 ft
(8848 m)

28,251 ft
(8611 m)

28,169 ft
(8586 m)

THE LONGEST RIVERS

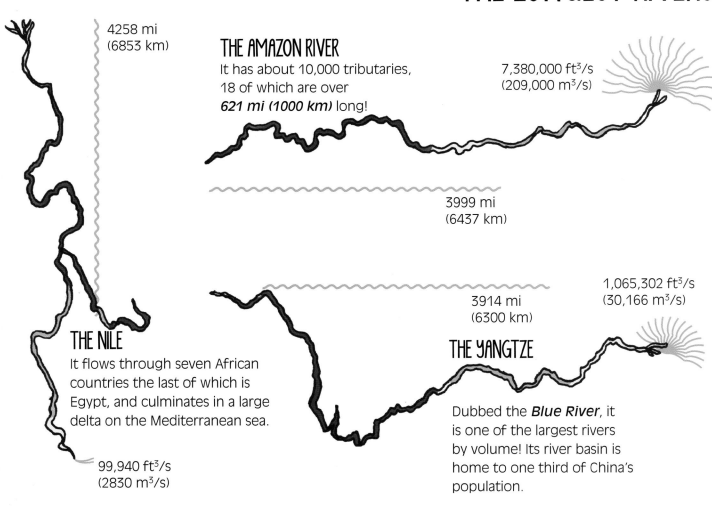

4258 mi
(6853 km)

THE AMAZON RIVER
It has about 10,000 tributaries, 18 of which are over **621 mi (1000 km)** long!

7,380,000 ft³/s
(209,000 m³/s)

3999 mi
(6437 km)

3914 mi
(6300 km)

1,065,302 ft³/s
(30,166 m³/s)

THE NILE
It flows through seven African countries the last of which is Egypt, and culminates in a large delta on the Mediterranean sea.

THE YANGTZE

Dubbed the **Blue River**, it is one of the largest rivers by volume! Its river basin is home to one third of China's population.

99,940 ft³/s
(2830 m³/s)

THE GIANTS AMONG THE VOLCANOES

At 20,960 ft (6390 m), close to the summit of this volcano, situated between the Chilean and the Argentinean borders there is *a lake*.

OJOS DEL SALADO

22,615 ft
(6893 m)

On its summit, *500-year-old mummies have been unearthed*. It marks the boundary between Chile and Argentina.

LLULLAILLACO

22,109 ft
(6739 m)

The last eruption of this Argentinian giant took place *about 10,000 years ago*.

CERRO TIPAS

21,850 ft
(6660 m)

understanding the symbols

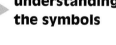 ~~~~~ *length*

 rate of flow

height | *depth*

● *area*

THE DEEPEST LAKES!

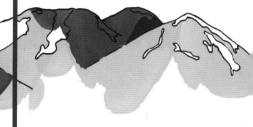 CASPIAN SEA

5370 ft
(1637 m)

12,250 mi²
(31,722 km²)

LAKE BAIKAL

It is estimated that this Siberian lake contains about *20% of all fresh water on the planet!*

LAKE TANGANYIKA

Over *450 species of fish live in this lake, which extends to the borders of Tanzania, Congo, Burundi and Zambia*.

4822 ft
(1470 m)

12,700 mi²
(32,900 km²)

3362 ft
(1025 m)

143,000 mi²
(371,000 km²)

Because of its large size, it is referred to as a *sea, but because of* its low salinity, it is classified as a lake.

speed

strength

height reached

THE FASTEST ANIMALS

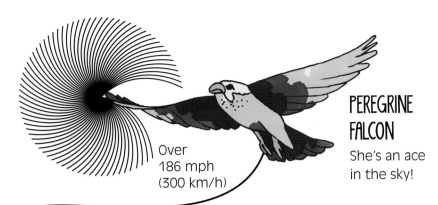

Over 186 mph (300 km/h)

PEREGRINE FALCON

She's an ace in the sky!

62 mi (100 km)

CHEETAH

The absolute *land speed record holder* in the Animal Kingdom.

SAILFISH

The *fastest* competitor *in the sea* is the sailfish: the water's density doesn't stop him!

68 mi (109 km)

595 lb (270 kg)

THE STRONGEST

AFRICAN ELEPHANT

RHINOCEROS BEETLE

2.9 lb (1.3 kg)

An elephant's *trunk* has about 100,000 muscles and it can lift weights!

It carries loads that are up to 850 times its weight!

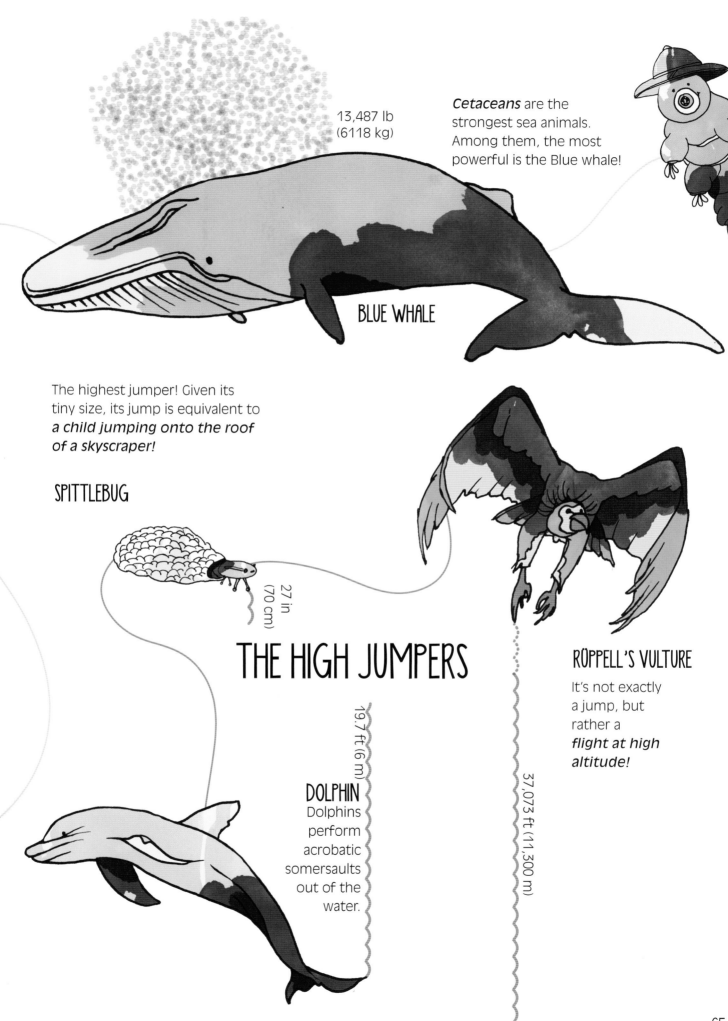

13,487 lb
(6118 kg)

Cetaceans are the strongest sea animals. Among them, the most powerful is the Blue whale!

BLUE WHALE

The highest jumper! Given its tiny size, its jump is equivalent to *a child jumping onto the roof of a skyscraper!*

SPITTLEBUG

27 in
(70 cm)

THE HIGH JUMPERS

RÜPPELL'S VULTURE

It's not exactly a jump, but rather a *flight at high altitude!*

19.7 ft (6 m)

37,073 ft (11,300 m)

DOLPHIN
Dolphins perform acrobatic somersaults out of the water.

WE, THE PLANET'S GUARDIANS

Because the Earth is our home, we need to nurture it.

The lack of care and respect for the environment can lead to dire consequences. Surely you are aware that the *pollution* caused by fossil fuels, industrial gases and landfill, has *detrimental effects* on the environment, such as rising sea levels, marine pollution, land degradation, and the melting of the polar ice caps!

Another great threat to our planet's health is *deforestation*, that is the destruction of the forests, which act as the green lungs of the Earth and play a key role in keeping the air that we breathe clean.
Until a few years ago *the Amazon forest*, one of the Planet's largest and most valuable ecosystems, was able to trap over 2 billion tons of carbon dioxide, an extremely toxic environmental pollutant. This impressive capacity is diminishing rapidly. Every year over *9266 mi² (24,000 km²) of rain forest are destroyed* and with it, more than 50,000 species of creatures living among its trees disappear.

Fortunately, not all human activity is detrimental
to the environment.

*Many organizations have sprung up with the
purpose of protecting our planet's health!*

The daily efforts of major, historical associations such
as the **National Geographic Society**, are essential
to counteract the effects of pollution on the Earth
and its inhabitants.

HAVE YOU EVER CONSIDERED THAT,
IN OUR OWN SMALL WAY, WE CAN ALL HELP
SAVE THE WORLD?

ALL IT TAKES IS A FEW, SIMPLE DAILY HABITS!

Here are some examples:

• Remember to turn off the TV or the Play Station at the switch, once you are finished using them: in standby mode they waste about 10% of electricity and a higher power consumption equals more environmental pollution.

• Turn off the faucet while brushing your teeth: in just a few minutes, you'll save about 30 bottles of water!

• Keep using your things, such as pens and coloring pencils until they are completely used up; that way, you'll notice that you buy less and therefore, produce less waste!

• If you feel like you've lost interest in your toys, wait before buying new ones. Use your imagination and your creativity! Try using jars, tins, boxes or cans to invent new ones! This is another way to avoid creating more waste!

• Utilize an entire sheet of paper before throwing it away, and use it on both sides: between notebooks and drawing paper, each family wastes about 2 trees a year!

• It's important to dispose of the drawing paper by using the correct recycling container: 2,2 lb (1 kg) of recycled paper is a tree saved!

• You know it takes the environment a very long time to eliminate waste; for this reason it's important to get rid of trash by always using the appropriate garbage can. Think about it: eliminating a chewing gum that has been thrown on the ground, takes 5 years! It takes 100 years for a can of drink, and up to 1000 to eliminate one plastic bag!

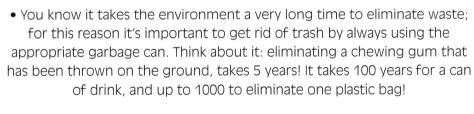

OUR JOURNEY ENDS HERE MY FRIEND,
NOW IT'S YOUR TURN!

Federica Fragapane

was born in Vercelli in 1988; she is a designer and freelance illustrator.
While studying at the Politecnico in Milan, she specialized in Information Design and data visualization, fields in which she has worked since 2012.
Her thesis was selected and published in the ADI Design Index 2015 under the Targa Giovani category, and one of her projects won an Honorable Mention at the *Kantar Information is Beautiful Awards 2014*. Over the years, she has worked with various publishing houses and magazines in Italy and abroad.

Chiara Piroddi

was born in Vercelli in 1982; she is a psychologist and expert in Neuropsychology, specializing in Cognitive-Evolutionary Psychotherapy. She graduated in Psychology at the University of Pavia in 2007 and continued as a teaching assistant for the Chair of Physiological Psychology, and as a lecturer in Practical Neuropsychology Training at the same academic institution. She completed her practical training at the Niguarda Ca' Granda Hospital in Milan, where she has worked since 2008, acquiring clinical experience in children with serious mental and physical disabilities of all ages. She is an author and co-author of several scientific publications on Neuropsychology.
An enthusiastic traveler with a curious soul, she lives between Barcelona and Milan, where he works as a psychotherapist in developmental age.

Graphic design
Valentina Figus

White Star Kids® is a trademark propriety of White Star s.r.l.

© 2016, 2018 White Star s.r.l.
Piazzale Luigi Cadorna, 6
20123 Milan, Italy
www.whitestar.it

Translation and Editing: Contextus Srl, Pavia, Italy
(Translation: Christine Guthry)

ISBN 978 88 544 1246 0
1 2 3 4 5 6 22 21 20 19 18

Printed in Croatia

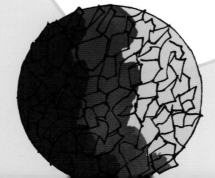